'*Listen for a Moment*'

A Small Book of Australian Ballads

Selected and introduced by
Tom Ford

National Library of Australia
Canberra 2000

Published by the National Library of Australia
Canberra ACT 2600
Australia

National Library of Australia Cataloguing-in-Publication entry

'Listen for a moment': a small book of Australian ballads.

ISBN 0 642 10722 X.

1. Ballads, English—Australia. 2. Folk songs—Australia.
3. Folk poetry, Australian. I. Ford, Tom. II. National
Library of Australia.

A821.0440894

Edited by Maureen Brooks
Designed by Kathy Jakupec
Printed by Inprint Limited, Brisbane

Front cover:
S.T. Gill (1818–1880)
Concert Room, Napier Hotel, Ballarat, June, '55,
Thatcher's Popular Songs 1855 (detail)

Contents

A Shearing Shed in 1883
Reproduced from the *Sydney Mail,* July–Dec 1883 (detail)

Introduction

There are few literary forms in which the difference between the spoken or sung text and the printed word is more marked than that of ballads. As A.B. Paterson wrote in the Introduction to his collection *Old Bush Songs*: 'these bush songs, to be heard at their best, should be heard to an accompaniment of clashing shears when the voice of the shearer rises through the din caused by the rush and bustle of a shearing shed, the scrambling of the sheep in their pens, and the hurry of the pickers-up; or when, on the roads, the cattle are restless in their camp at night and the man on watch, riding round them, strikes up "Bold Jack Donahoo" to steady their nerves a little.'

But few Australians now feel at home in the shearing sheds or round the camp fires where these ballads were once performed, and where they found their content and inspiration. The rhythm of collective physical labour— 'an accompaniment of clashing shears'—that gives these ballads their uneven yet insistent metre is not heard in the office, nor the shopping mall, nor indeed on many farms today. If these songs appear here stripped of their music, this reflects the sense in which they have been stripped of their context: while words on a page are a weak reflection of the original song, the original song often does not now exist. The recovery of a truly authentic performance of these songs is no longer possible, if only because those listening have changed so much.

One mark of the gap that separates us from these songs is the need for explanation; for knowledge that could once be assumed, but now needs to be supplied. Many of these songs contain references to topical events and figures; now these references often appear mysterious, their importance only evident when one turns to a book of history. But commentary, while it can illuminate, can also further distance the reader, emphasising the song's status as a historical artefact, a riddle from an alien past. Commentary here has been kept to a minimum; notes have been supplied where necessary, but do not appear for every ballad.

Despite this historical distance and the evanescent character of folklore, Australians still have access to these ballads, which document the history of Australian society and culture in a unique and powerful way. The National Library of Australia has one of the strongest collections of ballads and folk songs in its Oral History Collection, largely thanks to the efforts of individual collectors such as John Meredith, Norm O'Connor, Alan Scott and their colleagues. Recording singers, musicians and yarn-spinners on farms and in pubs and retirement homes, these collectors preserved the music and poetry of earlier generations that would otherwise be lost.

An important benefit of the depth of the Library's Collection is the preservation of 'odd' songs. While folk songs reveal history, that history is one filtered by the attitudes and experiences of the singers. That these songs express particular recurrent themes and attitudes is a consequence of their provenance in a predominantly male world—the rural workplace of the nineteenth century—and their dependence on an informal public sphere in which to spread. Seasonal and itinerant workers, such as sailors or shearers, could easily pick up new songs as they moved from job to job; until recently, few women enjoyed such freedom. But no tradition is wholly exclusive, and the Library's Collection holds songs that challenge these dominant attitudes, like D. Bouverie's 'The Ballad-Maker'. Similarly, the Library has large holdings of Aboriginal folk songs in English, such as Katie Martin's 'Stick Tight Bunny'—songs that express a very different history to that found in Paterson's *Old Bush Songs*.

If 'truly authentic' performances are now impossible, if these ballads only exist preserved in oral history collections or on the printed page, this does not mean that the tradition of ballads is dead. The use of song to present simple stories—comical, political, romantic, celebratory stories—remains very much a living tradition. The irreverent sense of humour and strong conviction in justice and honesty so evident in the songs collected in this book can still be detected in songs sung in pubs and workplaces, clubs and streets, all over Australia today. And in some ways, many modern Australian poems are complex responses to these folk poems, challenging yet continuing the various forms of Australianness represented in these first Australian ballads.

Thomas Rowlandson (1756–1827)
[Convicts embarking for Botany Bay] 180-?

Jim Jones at Botany Bay

O, listen for a moment lads, and hear me tell my tale—
How, o'er th' sea from England's shore I was compelled to sail.
The jury says 'he's guilty, sir,' and says the judge, says he—
'For life, Jim Jones, I'm sending you across the stormy sea;
And take my tip, before you ship to join the Iron-gang,
Don't be too gay at Botany Bay, or else you'll surely hang—
Or else you'll hang,' he says, says he—'and after that, Jim Jones,
High up upon the gallow-tree th' crows will pick your bones—
You'll have no chance for mischief then; remember what I say,
They'll flog th' poachin' out of you, out there at Botany Bay.'

The winds blew high upon th' sea, and th' pirates came along,
But the soldiers on our convict ship were full five hundred strong.
They opened fire and somehow drove that pirate ship away.
I'd have rather joined that pirate ship than come to Botany Bay:
For night and day the irons clang, and like poor galley slaves,
We toil, and toil, and when we die must fill dishonoured graves.
But bye-and-bye I'll break my chains: into the bush I'll go,
And join th' brave bushrangers there—Jack Donohoo and Co.;
And some dark night when everything is silent in the town
I'll kill the tyrants, one and all; and shoot th' floggers down:
I'll give th' Law a little shock: remember what I say,
They'll yet regret they sent Jim Jones in chains to Botany Bay.

James Reid Scott (1839–1877)
Flogging Prisoners, Tasmania c.1850

Moreton Bay

as sung by Simon McDonald

I am a native of the land of Erin;
I was early banished from my native shore;
On the ship Columbus went circular sailing,
And I left behind me the girl I adored.
O'er the bounding billows, which were loudly raging,
Like a bold sea mariner, my course did steer;
We were bound for Sydney, our destination,
And every day in irons wore.

When I arrived, 'twas in Port Jackson,
I thought my days would happy be;
But I found out I was greatly mistaken:
I was taken a prisoner to Moreton Bay.
Moreton Bay, you'll find no equal:
Norfolk Island, and Emu plains,
At Castle Hill, and cursed Toongabbie,
And all time places in New South Wales.

Now every morning as the day was dawning—
As we rose—from heaven fell the morning dew;
And we were roused without a moment's warning
Our daily labour to renew.
For three long years I was beastly treated
And heavy irons on my legs I wore;
My back from flogging was lacerated
And oft times painted with crimson gore.

Like the Egyptians and ancient Hebrews
We were oppressed under Logan's yoke;
But a native black there lay in ambush
Did give this tyrant a mortal stroke.
Now fellow prisoners, be exhilarated
That all such monsters such deaths may find;
And when from bondage we are liberated
Then our former sufferings shall fade from mind.

Moreton Bay, you'll find no equal:
Norfolk Island, and Emu plains,
At Castle Hill, and cursed Toongabbie,
And all time places in New South Wales.

Moreton Bay was established as a penal settlement in 1824; its purpose was to incarcerate convicts convicted of crimes in New South Wales—that is, repeat offenders. Captain Patrick Logan became commandant of Moreton Bay in March 1826 and soon gained a reputation for extreme cruelty. In 1830 he was killed, while surveying the upper Brisbane River. It was rumoured amongst convicts of the time that Logan had been killed by Aboriginal people sympathetic to their condition.

This song was probably written by Francis McNamara— 'Frank the Poet'—a convict transported from Ireland in 1832. Like other 'Frank the Poet' ballads, 'Moreton Bay' or 'The Convict's Lament' quickly entered folk tradition and exists in many variant versions; this version was recorded from Simon McDonald in 1960.

S.T. Gill (1818–1880)
Interior of John Alloo's Restaurant, Ballaarat 1855

Old Dog Tray

Charles Thatcher

But, unless my watch is fast,
  The morning time is past,
And to sing of the dawn, it's too late in the day;
  Yet I've tried a change of air,
  Almost more than I can bear—
It reminds me of my old dog Tray.

  Old dog Tray was ever faithful—
Grief came upon him though one day;
  For the governmental hacks
  Would insist upon his tax,
Which was fatal to my old dog Tray.

  He was very good at rats
  And a mortal foe to cats;
We were more like brothers than I care to say:
  But eight shillings every year
  For his company it was dear,
And there was nothing left of old dog Tray.

  Old dog Tray had a plateful
Of bones and potatoes one fine day;
  And inside the sav'ry mass hid
  Was a dose of prussic acid,
Which made an end of old dog Tray.

They bore him from my sight,
And it overcame me quite—
I was ill—I was wretched—I was wasting away;
From my food I loathing turned,
And my dinner beer I spurned;
Ah! thinking of my old dog Tray.

Old dog Tray, we met again though;
To eat they persuaded me one day,
With some tempting mutton pies,
In the which I recognised
The flavour of my old dog Tray.

Charles Thatcher (1831–1878) was a popular entertainer on the goldfields, writing and performing songs dealing with topical events; as the title of a contemporary collection of his song books states, his songs form 'a complete comic history of the early diggings'. This song concerns both the imposition of a tax on dogs in an effort to reduce dog numbers on the goldfields, and also, of course, the quality of food on the diggings.

Death of Ben Hall

as sung by Sally Sloane

Come, all you young Australians, and everyone besides,
I'll sing to you a ditty that will fill you with surprise,
Concerning of a 'ranger bold, whose name it was Ben Hall,
But cruelly murdered was this day, which proved his downfall.

An outcast from society, he was forced to take the road,
All through his false and treacherous wife, who sold off his abode.
He was hunted like a native dog from bush to hill and dale,
Till he turned upon his enemies and they could not find his trail.

All out with his companions, men's blood he scorned to shed,
He oft times stayed their lifted hands, with vengence on their heads.
No petty, mean or pilfering act he ever stooped to do,
But robbed the rich and hearty man, and scorned to rob the poor.

One night as he in ambush lay all on the Lachlan Plain,
When, thinking everything secure, to ease himself had lain,
When to his consternation and to his great surprise,
And without one moment's warning, a bullet past him flies.

And it was soon succeeded by a volley sharp and loud,
With twelve revolving rifles all pointed at his head.
'Where are you, Gilbert? Where is Dunn?' he loudly did call.
It was all in vain, they were not there to witness his downfall.

Although he had a lion's heart, more braver than the brave,
Those cowards shot him like a dog—no word of challenge gave.
Though many friends had poor Ben Hall, his enemies were few,
Like the emblems of his native land, his days were numbered too.

It's through Australia's sunny clime Ben Hall will roam no more.
His name will spread both near and far to every distant shore.
For generations after this parents will to their children call,
And rehearse to them the daring deeds committed by Ben Hall.

Patrick William Marony
Death of Ben Hall 1894

The Waterwitch

as sung by J.H. Davies

A neat little packet from Hobart set sail
For to cruise 'round the westward for monster sperm whales;
Cruise in the westward, where the stormy winds blow,
Bound away in the *Waterwitch*, to the west'd we go.

Bound away, bound away, where the stormy winds blow,
Bound away to the west'd in the *Waterwitch* we go.

Oh it's early one morning just as the sun rose;
A man from the masthead cries out: 'There she blows!'
'We're away!' cried the skipper, and springing aloft;
'Three points on the lee bow and scarce three miles off.

'Get your lines in your boats, my boys, see your box-line all clear,
And lower me down, my bully-boys, and after him we'll steer.
Now the ship, she gets full, my boys; to Hobart we steer,
Where there's plenty of pretty girls and plenty good beer.

'We'll spend our money freely with the pretty girls on shore,
And when it's all gone we'll go whaling for more.'
Bound away, bound away, where the stormy winds blow,
Bound away in the *Waterwitch*, to the west'd we go.

Opposite page: *Barque Waterwitch*
Reproduced from *Whalers Out of Van Diemen's Land*
ed. by Harry O'May
(Hobart: Government Printer, 195-)
Reproduced courtesy of the Printing Authority of Tasmania

The Waterwitch *was a whaling ship based in Hobart from 1860. Originally launched from the Pembroke naval dockyard as HMS* Falcon, *she was used as a slave-chaser off the coast of Africa before being bought and renamed by Hobart shipowner Alex McGregor. In* Whalers Out of Van Diemen's Land, *Harry O'May writes: 'The* Witch, *as she was known locally, was a weatherly vessel, and was one of the very few that could beat to windward with a whale lashed alongside ... [In 1893]* Waterwitch *came in after eight month's voyage under Captain W. Folder, with 52 tuns of oil. She had had a boat smashed by the flick of a whale's tail. The old barque, still under the blue and white gridiron flag of Alex McGregor, was earning very satisfactory dividends.' The* Waterwitch *made her last voyage in 1895, the second-last whaler to sail out of Hobart.*

[Kanaka Labourers on a Queensland Pineapple Plantation] (detail)
photograph

Sam Griffith

as sung by Jack Luscombe

One night while lying in my bunk in my humble six by eight,
I dreamt I saw Sam Griffith with a darkie for a mate;
I thought I met them travelling on a dreary Queensland track,
And Sam was decorated with a collar-fashioned pack.

I thought that it was summertime; and Sam had o'er his eyes
A little piece of muslin to protect him from the flies.
Through his boots his toes were shining, and his feet looked very sore—
I knew his heels were blistered from the Alberts that he wore.

When Sam saw me coming towards them he sat down upon his swag.
Said he: 'Good morning, stranger, got much water in your bag?
We're victimised by squatters for we are two union men.'
And Sam had on as usual his same old polished grin.

Said I: 'Look here, Sammy Griffith, you have a flamin' cheek.
If you want a drink of water you can get it from the creek.
As for the South Sea Islander, I do not wish him ill;
For well I know, poor devil, he's here against his will.

'You said, with wife and family one time you'd emigrate
If they did not stop Kanakas—that was in eighty-eight.
You spoke against black labour then and talked of workers' rights.
You spoke from lips but not from heart—Australia for the whites.

'You should loaf to those you crawl to, the sugar-growing push,
For you're hated and detested by the workers in the bush.
They might give you some easy billets, such as boots and shoes to clean,
Or driving the Kanakas as they work amongst the cane.'

I thought Sam jumped up, froth around his mouth like spray.
Said he: 'My agitator, just let me have a say.
I remember you at Longreach, how you did hoot and groan.
I believe you would have mobbed me but for Constable Malone.'

I thought Sam tried to rush me and shape before my face.
But I got home the La Blanche swing and gave him coup de grâce.
The darkie raised his tomahawk, and gave a savage scream;
And all at once I wakened up and found it all a dream.

This topical song concerns Sir Samuel Griffith (1845–1920),
who was premier of Queensland from 1883 to 1888 and from
1890 to 1893. One of the central political issues of Griffiths'
premiership was blackbirding, a form of slavery in which
Polynesian islanders, or Kanakas, were kidnapped and made to
work on Queensland canefields and farms for minimal wages.
Originally an opponent of blackbirding, Griffiths passed a Bill
outlawing the importation of Kanakas in 1890; however, as this
song notes, he reneged from this position in 1892 under pressure
from the sugar industry, and the practice continued until
Federation.

Griffith was the target of further hostility from the labour
movement for his actions during the recession of the 1890s,
when he employed the military to track and arrest strikers.
Jack Luscombe, who sang this song for John Meredith in 1953,
had taken part in the shearers' strike at Longreach in 1891, and
his comments on the tensions of the time are on tape at the
National Library. Later in his career Griffith played a
significant role in the drafting of Australia's constitution and
became the first Chief Justice of the High Court.

'Alberts' refer to Prince Alberts—strips of cloth or sacking
wound around the feet and worn by swagmen instead of socks.

A 'collar-fashioned pack' is a type of swag.

The Stockman

A bright sun and a loosened rein,
      A whip whose pealing sound
Rings forth amid the forest trees
      As merrily forth we bound—
As merrily forth we bound, my boys,
      And, by the dawn's pale light,
Speed fearless on our horses true
      From morn till starry night.

'Oh! for a tame and quiet herd.'
      I hear some crawler cry;
But give to me the mountain mob
      With the flash of their tameless eye—
With the flash of their tameless eye, my boys,
      As down the rugged spur
Dash the wild children of the woods,
      And the horse that mocks at fear.

There's mischief in yon wide-horned steer,
      There's danger in yon cow;
Then mount, my merry horsemen all,
      The wild mob's bolting now—
The wild mob's bolting now, my boys,
      But 'twas never in their hides
To show the way to the well-trained nags
      That are rattling by their sides.

Oh! 'tis jolly to follow the roving herd
  Through the long, long summer day,
And camp at night by some lonely creek
  When dies the golden ray.
When the jackass laughs in the old gum tree,
  And our quart-pot tea we sip;
The saddle was our childhood's home,
  Our heritage the whip.

Samuel Calvert (1828–1913)
Mustering Cattle on the Bogong High Plains: A Rough Customer 1892

This ballad, reproduced from the Queenslander *(an illustrated weekly paper published between 1866 and 1939) is clearly a more 'literary' production than the other ballads presented here. The metre is quite regular; the language recalls English poetic models that sit rather oddly with the subject (for instance, in the phrase 'yon wide-horned steer'); and it has never been recorded in oral tradition. The 'literary' ballad, best known from the work of poets such as Henry Kendall or Adam Lindsay Gordon, emerged in the second half of the nineteenth century as Australian daily life came to be seen as a fit subject for poetry. However, tensions between subject and poetic means were not relieved until colloquial vocabulary became an accepted form of poetic expression with writers such as Henry Lawson and Paterson himself—ironically, a shift strongly influenced by British poets such as Tennyson and the 'poet of Empire', Rudyard Kipling.*

D. Bouverie's 'The Ballad-Maker' offers a sharp riposte to this type of 'bush song', challenging the ways in which literary balladists represented Australian life. While 'The Stockman' is a rural, masculine figure, Bouverie comically presents the writers of poems like 'The Stockman' as urban and dominated by women: the gap between subject and language then mimics the gap between the reality and the poetic fiction.

Edward Roper (c.1830–1904)
Yarding Stock for Branding: An Old Scrubber c.1855 (detail)

Alf Vincent, illustrator (1874–1915)
The Ballad-Maker 1905
Reproduced from the *Bulletin* (Sydney), 14 December 1905

The Ballad-Maker

D. Bouverie

Ho! The Ballad-writer rose, snorting slaughter down his nose
And he drew his pen as though it were a sword:
And he dashed it in the ink, nor a moment paused to think
As the livid lines across the page he scored.

Now he wrote of blood and death while his sulphurated breath
Made the letters dance with tiny flames of blue,
And his greenish rolling eyes, glaring twice their usual size,
Peopled vacancy with warriors strong and true.

''Ow much longer will yer be, comin' down to 'ave yer tea?
Whoi the mischief can't ye come down when ye're towld?
It is standin' in the pot—come an' 'ave it while it's 'ot
An' the sossidges are very nearly cowld.'

'Yes, I'm coming now my dear,' gasped the poet blanched with fear,
And the eye that lately flamed was soft and weak—
In those accents loud and shrill spoke a warrior woman's will—
And to tea there slunk a poet, mild and meek.

Antarctic Fleet

as sung by Harry Robertson

I went down South a-whaling to the land of ice and snow;
And eight-and-twenty pounds a month was all I had to show,
For living on the little ship like a sardine in the can
And eating salty pork and beef that's chewed up in the pan.

Chorus—Hey-ho, Whale-Oh, we're the Antarctic fleet.
I've got a drip upon my nose and I'm frozen in the feet.

South Georgia is an island; it is a whaling base;
And only men in search of whales would go to such a place.
No entertainment does exist unless you make home-brew,
Then we will have some singing and no doubt some fighting too.

The gunner came from Norway, like many of the crew,
And others spoke with Scottish tongues, as whalers often do;
But when the ship was closing in to make the bloody kill
The Scotsmen and Norwegians were together with a will.

We sailed into the Weddell Sea, where the big blues can be found,
We chased between the icebergs and we chased them round and round;
And when they couldn't run no more, and fought to draw their breath,
The gunner shot harpoons in them till they floated still in death.

For months we sailed the ocean and wearied with the toil
Of slaughter and of killing just to get that smelly oil;
And when the savage storms blew and snow kept falling down
I often wished that I was back in dear old Glasgow town.

It's plenty year since I've been there, and I won't go there again:
I didn't like the climate but I liked the whaling men.
And even in the sunshine now when I walk along the street
I've got a drip upon my nose and I've still got frozen feet.

Hey-ho, Whale-Oh, we're the Antarctic fleet.
I've got a drip upon my nose and I'm frozen in the feet.

Oswald Brierly (1817–1894)
The Death Flurry 1865

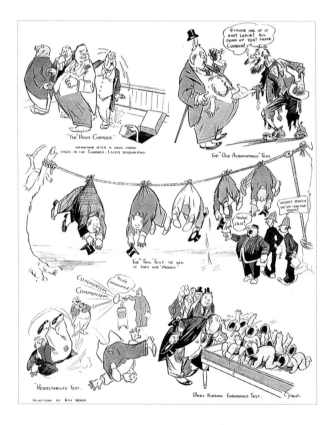

Joseph Lynch, illustrator
The Testing
Reproduced from the *Melbourne Punch*, 12 November 1925

Bump Me Into Parliament

'Written by Casey'

Come listen, all kind friends of mine
    I want to move a motion;
To make an Eldorado here
    I've got a bonzer notion.

Chorus—Bump me into Parliament,
    Bounce me any wa—y
Bang me into Parliament
    On next election day.

Some very wealthy friends I know
    Declare I am most clever.
While some may talk for an hour or so,
    Why, I can talk for ever.

I know the Arbitration Act
    As a sailor knows his 'riggins':
So if you want a small advance
    I'll talk to Justice Higgins.

Oh yes, I am a Labor man
    And believe in revolution;
The quickest way to bring them on
    Is talking constitution.

To keep the cost of living down
    A law I straight would utter,
A hundred loaves for a tray I'd sell
    With a penny a ton for butter.

They say that kids are getting scarce,
  I believe there's something in it;
By extra laws I'd incubate
  A million kids a minute.

I've read my library ten times through
  And Wisdom justifies me.
The man who does not vote for me
  By Cripes, he crucifies me.

 Now Sinclair, he was fined five quid
  For singing this here ditty;
Betsy was his witness there
  But the 'Bobby' pooled the 'Kitty.'

So—Bump 'em into Parliament,
  Bounce 'em any way;
Bang 'em into Parliament
  Don't let the Court decay.

This broad satire on parliamentary democracy probably dates from the 1910s, although the version published here is reproduced from a song book of the Industrial Labour Party from the 1920s. There it is described as 'sung to the tune of Yankee Doodle'.

Henry Higgins (1851–1929) was president of the Commonwealth Court of Conciliation and Arbitration between 1906 and 1920.

Katie Martin
photograph
Reproduced courtesy of Estelle Bertossi

Stick Tight Bunny

as sung by Katie Martin

Stick tight bunny,
But don't let him throw you;
Wany'ma'ri'gun lookin'.
Stick tight bunny.

But you ride him loose rein,
And you'll find it lot easy;
You take it from me.

On the Library's recording, Katie Martin prefaces this song with a short explanation: 'There was a man riding a horse, see, and this young man got on the horse, and the elderly man who couldn't ride said—trying to give him a few lessons—said: "Stick tight bunny, don't have him throw you; all the white women are looking at you."'

In the first verse Martin uses the Aboriginal language word wany'ma'ri'gun *which is the word for 'white woman' in the language of the Butchulla people from Fraser Island, Queensland.*

William Strutt (1825–1915)
[Study for Bushrangers, Victoria, Australia] 1852

The Ballad Trap

Les Murray

In the hanging gorges
The daring compact wears thin,
Picking meat from small skeletons,
Counting damp notes in a tin,

The rifle birds ringing at noon
In the steep woods,
Hard-riding boys dazed at the brink
Of their attitudes,

The youngest wheedling for songs,
His back to the night,
Dark mountains the very English
For souring delight:

Remember the Escort? Remember ...
Lamps long ago
And manhood filched from the horse police
And a name from Cobb and Co.

Their metre hobbled, the horses
Hump their dark life,
Longing for marriage, the tall man
Sharpens his knife—

Yes, let us sing! cries the Captain
While we have breath.
Better, God knows, than this thinking.
The ballad ends with their death.

Joseph Swain (1820–1909)
Australian Diggers Keeping Christmas Eve—Auld Lang Syne 1873 (detail)

References

Jim Jones at Botany Bay
from Charles MacAlister, *Old Pioneering Days in the Sunny South*. Goulburn: Chas. MacAlister Book Publication Committee, 1907

Moreton Bay
Simon McDonald (1907–1968), 1960, Norm O'Connor Collection, Oral History Collection, National Library of Australia

Old Dog Tray
from Charles Thatcher, *Thatcher's Colonial Minstrel: New Collection of Songs by the Inimitable Thatcher*. Melbourne: Charlwood and Son, 1864

Ben Hall
Sally Sloane (1894–1982), 195-?, John Meredith Collection, Oral History Collection, National Library of Australia

The Waterwitch
J.H. Davies (born 1873), c.1962, Norm O'Connor Collection, Oral History Collection, National Library of Australia

Sam Griffith
Jack Luscombe (born 1873), 1953, John Meredith Collection, Oral History Collection, National Library of Australia

The Stockman
from the *Queenslander* (Brisbane), 28 July 1894

The Ballad-Maker
D. Bouverie, from the *Bulletin* (Sydney), 28 July 1905

Antarctic Fleet
Harry Robertson (1923–1995), 196-?, Norm O'Connor
Collection, Oral History Collection, National Library of
Australia
Published with the permission of Rita Robertson

Bump Me Into Parliament
'Written by Casey, of the One Big Union League,
Melbourne', *Songs of the ILP*. Sydney: Industrial Labour
Party, 192-?

Stick Tight Bunny
Katie Martin (1910–1966), 195-?, Oral History Collection,
National Library of Australia
Published with the permission of Estelle Bertossi

The Ballad Trap
from Les Murray, *The Weatherboard Cathedral: Poems by
Les A. Murray*. Sydney: Angus & Robertson, 1969
Reproduced courtesy of Les Murray, c/– Margaret Connolly
& Associates Pty Ltd